THE
JOURNEY
THROUGH
GRIEF

Remember the past...
Hope for the future

Alan Wolfelt

10-97

Carolyn —
For those
Beautiful
"Addie"
moments.
Love Ya —
— Donna —

Also by Alan Wolfelt:

A Child's View of Grief

Creating Meaningful Funeral Ceremonies:
A Guide for Caregivers

Healing the Bereaved Child:
Grief Gardening, Growth Through Grief and Other
Touchstones for Caregivers

How to Care for Yourself While You Care
for the Dying and the Bereaved

How to Reach Out for Help When You are Grieving

How to Start and Lead a
Bereavement Support Group

Sarah's Journey

Understanding Grief: Helping Yourself Heal

Companion Press is dedicated to the education
and support of both the bereaved and bereavement
caregivers. We believe that those who companion the
bereaved by walking with them as they journey in grief
have a wondrous opportunity: to help others embrace and
grow through grief—and to lead fuller, more deeply-lived
lives themselves because of this important work.

For a complete catalog and ordering
information, write or call:

Companion Press
The Center for Loss and Life Transition
3735 Broken Bow Road
Fort Collins, CO 80526
(970) 226-6050

THE

JOURNEY
THROUGH
GRIEF

REFLECTIONS
ON HEALING

ALAN D. WOLFELT, PH.D.

Companion
PRESS

An imprint of the Center for
Loss and Life Transition

Fort Collins, Colorado

Companion Press is an imprint of the
Center for Loss and Life Transition,
3735 Broken Bow Road, Fort Collins, Colorado 80526.

Printed in the United States of America

06 05 04 03 02 01 00 99 98 97   5 4 3 2 1

ISBN: 1-879651-11-4

*To my parents, Don and Virgine Wolfelt.
Without your love and modeling of
compassionate care, my body of work in
grief would never have evolved.
I have been blessed to have you in my life.
I thank you for nurturing me in ways that
helped me learn the importance of
being present to people in pain.*

Contents

The Journey Through Grief:

A Prologue

The death of someone loved changes our lives forever. And the movement from the "before" to the "after" is almost always a long, painful journey. From my own experiences with loss as well as those of the thousands of grieving people I have companioned over the years, I have learned that if we are to heal we cannot skirt the outside edges of our grief. Instead, we must journey all through it, sometimes meandering the side roads, sometimes plowing directly into its raw center.

I have also learned that the journey requires mourning. There is an important difference, you see. Grief is what you think and feel on the inside after someone you love dies. Mourning is the outward expression of those thoughts and feelings. To mourn is to be an active participant in our grief journeys. We all grieve when someone we love dies, but if we are to heal, we must also mourn.

This series of reflections is but one small attempt to encourage you to journey all through your very unique and personal grief—to help you, when you are ready, gently embrace your need to mourn so that you may heal. Perhaps you can think of this book and these reflections as an invitation — an invitation to mourn!

Why a series of reflections? Because another important lesson I have learned is that healing in grief is heart-based, not head-based. Modern therapies sometimes separate the head from the heart; it's as if we should somehow be able to rationally think through our grief. Yet it was Carl Jung who taught us that every psychological

1

struggle is ultimately a matter of spirituality. The reflections in this book encourage you to think, yes, but to think with your heart and your soul. They invite you to go to that spiritual place inside you and, transcending our mourning-avoiding society and even your own personal inhibitions about grief, enter deeply into the journey.

This book also describes six "yield signs" you are likely to encounter on your journey through grief—what I call the "needs of mourning":

1. Acknowledging the reality of the death;
2. Embracing the pain of the loss;
3. Remembering the person who died;
4. Developing a new self-identity;
5. Searching for meaning;
6. Receiving ongoing support from others.

For while your grief journey will be an intensely personal, unique experience, all mourners must yield to this set of basic human needs if they are to heal. In fact, your grief journey will be shaped by your innate compulsion to explore (and sometimes veer away from) each of these needs.

You will note that the needs of mourning are numbered 1-6. This is not meant to imply that your grief journey will be an orderly procession toward healing. If you are like most mourners, you will encounter the needs of mourning in random fashion. You will also likely find yourself working on more than one need at once. This is normal. When you pick up this book as you journey through grief, turn to the pages that seem most pertinent. We are accustomed to reading books front to back, but like grief, this book has no unbreechable sequence.

Neither does this book claim to teach you what your journey through grief should be like. The reflections on grief contained here come from my journeys both as a mourner and as a companion to thousands of people who have encountered the death of someone loved. Some may not speak to your unique journey. Some may even run counter to your experience. Take from this book only what is useful to you and ignore the rest.

I would, however, like you to think of reading this book as a form of caring for yourself during this difficult time. Self-care when we are grieving is essential to our survival. For it is in nurturing ourselves—in allowing ourselves the time and loving attention we need to journey through our grief—that we find meaning in our continued living. It is in having the courage to care for our own needs that we discover a fullness to living and loving again.

Before you read this book, you may want to find a safe, quiet place where you can be alone with your thoughts. You might even want to read the reflective passages aloud, for speaking the words seems to make them more real. In the weeks and months ahead, you may want to revisit this book as you find your journey taking you to a new part of your grief, prodding you to rethink and refeel all that has come before.

Right now you have special needs that must be tended to. I hope you make use of this book as one way of helping yourself heal. If you find these reflections helpful, perhaps you can pass this book on to others and encourage them to mourn well, so they can live well, and love well.

Alan D. Wolfelt

MOURNING NEED

1

ACKNOWLEDGING THE REALITY OF THE DEATH

You can know something in your head but not in your heart. This is what often happens when someone you love dies. This first need of mourning involves gently confronting the reality that someone you care about will never physically come back into your life again.

Whether the death was sudden or anticipated, acknowledging the full reality of the loss may occur over weeks and months. You may expect him or her to come through the door, to call on the telephone, or even to touch you. To survive, you may try to push away the reality of the death at times. But to know that someone you love has died is done in "doses;" embracing this painful reality is not quick, easy or efficient.

You may move back and forth between protesting and encountering the reality of the death. You may discover yourself replaying events surrounding the death and confronting memories, both good and bad. This replay is a vital part of this need of mourning. It's as if each time you talk it out, the event is a little more real.

One moment the reality of the loss may be tolerable; another moment it may be unbearable. Be patient with this need. At times you may feel like running away and hiding. At other times you may hope you will awake from what seems like a bad dream. As you express what you think and feel outside of yourself, you will be working on this important need.

Remember—this first need of mourning, like the other five that follow, may intermittently require your attention for months. Be patient and compassionate with yourself as you work on each of them.

The reality of this death demands my attention. As I move from head understanding to heart understanding, I know with burning certainty that life is forever changed. I arrive at this new place unprepared for the journey ahead. How will I set forth?

*While embracing the reality of
this death is painful beyond words, the
more I open myself to allowing small
doses of reality in, the more
I open my heart to healing.*

*I understand that allowing the full
reality of this death to enter my head
and heart is a source of necessary hurt.
While I do not seek the hurt, I seek
the healing. Once I understand that,
the pain actually begins to dissolve.
Yes, I still hurt, but the depth of
the pain will ease over time.*

*Little by little, step by step,
I realize that seeking protection
by evading some of the reality of this
death helps me survive, at least for
now. But gently opening myself to the
reality ultimately offers the greatest
gift of all—the opportunity to
mourn so I can live again.*

*It's as if the realness of what has
happened waits around a corner.
I don't want to make the turn, yet
I know I must. Slowly, I gather
the courage to approach.*

To live into the future depends on my response to the reality of what I am experiencing. Temporarily, I need to create insulation from the full force of what I am coming to know. If I felt it all at once, I might die. But feel it I must—gently and in doses.

Taking time to turn inward and slow down helps me move from head to heart—a realization that is necessary, yet painful. Taking slow, deep breaths, I encourage my body to go into neutral.

*Acknowledging reality brings pain.
It is not instinctive to confront the
death of someone I love; I do
not want it to be so.*

*As I open myself to feel the total
sense of loss, I discover I cannot do
this grief work alone. I will need
the love and support of those who
understand the depths of this journey.
Most of all I will need to be around
people who are truly compassionate.*

I cannot begin to heal until I give in.
I cannot understand what is
happening until I free my heart from
the need to push away the reality.
I turn my head and my heart
toward my grief.

There is something extraordinary
in my capacity to survive.
I must trust in the struggle.

The head, the heart and the soul must all come to embrace the reality of the death. It is the soul that gives life to the head and heart. I may know the reality of the death in my head but I must also let it sift down into my heart and soul. This is between me and my God.

In committing myself to my grief work, my mind may respond with fear and resistance. If I allow this resistance to overpower me, I will cut off the force that will ultimately help me heal.

Denial is a powerful, seductive force. As I confront it, what seems to help me is to stay focused on my grief work. It is through the encounter of my deep sense of loss that I stay connected to my innermost self.

*Encountering the reality of
death brings me to understand
that love is life. Love nourishes
the soul and brings meaning to my
life. As I realize this person I have
loved cannot come back, I am
transformed by my grief. Just as love
transforms us, so too does grief.*

*Perhaps the question is:
How will I be transformed?*

*It is tempting to put off this work
of grief; postponing or suppressing
it would be safer, less hurtful.
Yet the time is now! I must
embrace the uncertainty.*

*Instead of thinking I need to get
back to the "old normal," perhaps
I need to embrace how I am changed
forever by the death of someone loved.
To do this I have to acknowledge the
reality of the death and be willing to
connect to the deepest parts of
myself. That's when grief becomes
a growth process that transcends
the turmoil of change. I am new;
I am changed; I am reborn.*

MOURNING NEED

2

EMBRACING THE PAIN OF THE LOSS

This need of mourning requires us to embrace the pain of our loss—something we naturally don't want to do. It is easier to avoid, repress or deny the pain of grief than it is to confront it, yet it is in confronting our pain that we learn to reconcile ourselves to it. To heal we must go to the wilderness of our souls.

You will probably discover that you need to "dose" yourself in embracing your pain. In other words, you cannot (nor should you try to) overload yourself with the hurt all at one time. Sometimes you may need to distract yourself from the pain of death, while at other times you will need to create a safe place to move toward it.

Feeling your pain can sometimes zap you of your energy. When your energy is low, you may be tempted to suppress your grief or even run from it. If you start running and keep running, you may never heal. Dose your pain: yes! Deny your pain: no!

Unfortunately, our culture tends to encourage the denial of pain. We misunderstand the role of suffering. If you openly express your feelings of grief, misinformed friends may advise you to "carry on" or "keep your chin up." If, on the other hand, you remain "strong" and "in control," you may be congratulated for "doing well" with your grief. Actually, doing well with your grief means becoming well acquainted with your pain. Don't let others deny you this critical mourning need.

27

As you encounter your pain, you will also need to nurture yourself physically, emotionally and spiritually. Eat well, rest often and exercise regularly. Find others with whom you can share your painful thoughts and feelings; friends who listen without judging are your most important helpers as you work on this mourning need. Give yourself permission to question your faith. It's OK to be angry with God and to struggle with "meaning of life" issues at this time.

Never forget that grief work is done in "doses," not quickly and efficiently. Your pain will probably ebb and flow for months, even years; embracing it when it washes over you will require patience, support and strength.

Remember—our culture tends to have the shortest social norms for mourning of any culture in the world—we are given three days off work and expected to return to the routine. Be compassionate with yourself and know that the symptoms of your pain of grief mean you are trying to mourn. And to mourn is to heal!

In some ways, love and grief are
very much alike. They both have
the power to forever change our lives.
Just as I must surrender to love,
I must surrender to my grief.

In part, grief work means surrendering to something more powerful than myself. Without surrender there is no change in this pain I feel. As I give in, I begin to breathe in new life.

Hidden on the other side of the pain is universal love and acceptance of myself and others.

I may try to protect myself from my sadness by not talking about my loss. I may even secretly hope that the person who died will come back if I don't talk about it. Yet, as difficult as it is, I must feel it to heal it.

Trying to protect myself by denying my pain will only lead to more pain. I need to be honest with myself about my feelings and my needs.

The pain of grief, though natural and necessary, is so very draining. But pain is also a signal, a warning to listen to myself and to honor my needs. While I may react to my pain with anger, it may actually be my friend.

When my grief becomes overwhelming, I can restore myself by pulling in. I owe it to myself to honor my alone time. Meditation, solitude, quietness—these times restore me. Some of my best healing can be done in solitude.

Grief creates a natural disorientation—a kind of emotional and spiritual wilderness. In loss comes a period of emptiness, aloneness—new life has not yet emerged. As I commit myself to find healing, I am led to a deeper understanding of myself and a longing to return to the world around me.

*As I allow myself to mourn, I create
an opening in my heart. Releasing
the tensions of grief, surrendering
to the struggle, means freeing
myself to go forward.*

Surrendering to my grief means allowing myself to feel. It's about trusting in my capacity to come out on the other side of my overwhelming hurt. Instead of defending against my pain, I must release myself to the flow of experiencing it.

*Over time, this pain softens and
points the way toward healing.
As I surrender to the struggle, I become
more clear about my pathway. I must
bow to the pain and open my heart.*

*The only way to the other side is to
transcend my intellect and keep my
heart open wide.*

*Sometimes I may react to the pain
of grief with anger. Over time and with
supportive companions, I come
to see my pain not as a curse placed
on me but as a necessary response to
my loss. My pain is a symptom of
the need to turn toward myself
and seek understanding.*

*How can I learn to see my pain
as friend, not foe?*

I don't have to go in search of the pain of grief—it finds me. It's when I deny or insulate myself from the pain of the loss that I shut down. Ironically, it is in being open to the pain that I move through it to renewed living.

*The grief within me has its own
heartbeat. It has its own life, its
own song. Part of me wants to resist
the rhythms of my grief. Yet, as I
surrender to the song, I learn to
listen deep within myself.*

*Let the life of this journey be just
what it is—confusing, complicated,
at times overwhelming. I must keep
opening and changing through it all
until I become the unique person
who has transcended the pain and
discovered self-compassion—
a vulnerable yet grounded me who
chooses to live again.*

MOURNING
NEED

3

REMEMBERING
THE PERSON
WHO DIED

Do you have any kind of relationship with someone when they die? Of course. You have a relationship of memory. Precious memories, dreams reflecting the significance of the relationship and objects that link you to the person who died (such as photos, symbols, etc.) are examples of some of the things that give testimony to a different form of a continued relationship. This need of mourning involves allowing and encouraging yourself to pursue this relationship.

The process of beginning to embrace your memories often begins with the funeral. The ritual offers you an opportunity to remember the person who died and helps to affirm the value of the life that was lived. The memories you embrace during the time of the funeral set the tone for the changed nature of the relationship.

Embracing your memories can be a very slow and, at times, painful process that occurs in small steps. Remember—don't try to do all of your work of mourning at once. Go slowly and be patient with yourself.

But some people may try to take your memories away. Trying to be helpful, they encourage you to take down all the photos of the person who died. They tell you to keep busy or even to move out of your house. You, too, may think avoiding memories would be better for you. And why not? You are living in a culture that teaches you that to move away from—instead of toward—your grief is best.

In my experience, remembering the past makes hoping for the future possible. Your future will become open to new experiences only to the extent that you embrace the past.

Remembering the person I have loved allows me to slowly heal. Healing does not mean I will forget. Actually, it means I will remember. Gently, I will move forward, never forgetting my past.

*Memories may be good or bad
or in between, but in all cases they
seek to be embraced. Each memory
can be savored as unique, reflecting
how the person who is now
dead impacted my life.*

*By understanding the preciousness of
memories, I can embrace the way
I live my life. Each day I live is a
memory in the making. I have the
privilege to seize each moment,
to live until I too die.*

*Embracing memories of those who
have died helps me understand the
true value of time. I must remember to
let others know I love and cherish
them as gifts from God.*

*The essence of finding meaning
in the future is not to forget my past,
as I have been told, but instead to
embrace my past. For it is in listening
to the music of the past that I can
sing in the present and dance
into the future.*

I realize my memories are like deeply rooted flowers, grounded in beauty and embraced by nature. Just as flowers instinctively grow and flourish, so too can my memories.

*If I experience disorienting symptoms
of grief I do not understand, I can
listen to my soul and look for the
spaces of memories in my heart.
My memories contain the seeds
of my healing.*

My memories, especially those that have imprinted my heart, stay with me forever. My five senses have taken in my memories and made them a part of me; they are always available to my gaze. All I need to do is look for them.

I am the curator of my memories. As curator, I care for my memories with love and gratitude.

Memories, precious as they are, need meditation, acceptance and close embrace. As I nurture my memories, I nurture myself and those around me.

*My capacity to love and be loved
makes my heart fertile with memories
and images. These images cannot be
pushed away, but must be considered
bright lights shining upon me.*

As I remember those I have loved, I realize I will never tire of embracing the same events over and over again.

As I reflect on memories, I discover a depth of meaning even in the most simple events. Memories allow me to care for my heart.

As I reflect on the past, I may have a multitude of feelings—some good, some bad, some indifferent. This looking back is an important part of ultimately looking forward again.

I must be on the alert for those who feel threatened by the need to look to the past. For only through reviewing what was can I create what is, and what will be.

Memories—sometimes painful, often comforting—nestle against my soul and ache for expression.

My memories are an affair of the heart. Some are fresh and warm, while some are blocked from my present awareness. Without a doubt, my continued living is connected to my most heartfelt memories.

I can release the pain that touches my memories, but only if I remember them. I can release my grief, but only if I express it. Memories and grief must have a heart to hold them.

*Memories are my treasures—they carry
my story, my song, my light.
As I long for peace, I carry my memory
torch with me, a vital link in
the chain of humanity.*

MOURNING
NEED

4

DEVELOPING
A NEW
SELF-IDENTITY

Your personal identity, or self-perception, is the result of the ongoing process of establishing a sense of who you are. Part of your self-identity comes from the relationships you have with other people. When someone with whom you have a relationship dies, your self-identity, or the way you see yourself, naturally changes.

You may have gone from being a "wife" or "husband" to a "widow" or "widower." You may have gone from being a "parent" to a "bereaved parent." The way you define yourself and the way society defines you is changed.

A death often requires you to take on new roles that had been filled by the person who died. After all, someone still has to take out the garbage, someone still has to buy the groceries, someone still has to balance the checkbook. You confront your changed identity every time you do something that used to be done by the person who died. This can be very hard work and, at times, can leave you feeling very drained of emotional, physical and spiritual energy.

You may occasionally feel child-like as you struggle with your changing identity. You may feel a temporarily heightened dependence on others as well as feelings of helplessness, frustration, inadequacy and fear. These feelings can be overwhelming and scary, but they are actually a natural response to this important need of mourning.

Remember—do what you need to do in order to survive, for now, as you try to re-anchor yourself. To be dependent on others as you struggle with a changed identity does not make you bad or inferior. Your self-identity has been assaulted. Be compassionate with yourself. Accept the support of others.

Many people discover that as they work on this need, they ultimately discover some positive aspects of their changed self-identities. You may develop a renewed confidence in yourself, for example. You may develop a more caring, kind and sensitive part of yourself. You may develop an assertive part of your identity that empowers you to go on living even though you continue to feel a sense of loss.

Grief work fills up my heart and demands my every attention. I come to know myself in ways I never knew existed. Much of this transformation comes from taking my new understanding of the importance of love and relationships and integrating it into my everyday life.

Gradually I am finding there is no division between my grief work and my life work. I discover the essence of who I truly am through this transforming journey of grief.

As I search for who I am without the
person I love, I may feel uniquely
alone—like no one else in the world.
Yes, I may be different than other
mourners, but I am also very
much the same.

We share the pain of loss, the need
to embrace memories, the desire to
rediscover the whys of living. While
we are unique, we are one.
We are more like others than
we are different from them.

Today I will look for both the
"unique I" and the "group we."

Healing my grief is not in the future, it is in the here and now. As my heart opens to the pain, part of me wants to pull away and hide from the very emotions that are part of the experience. It is in this lived-through experience that I am transformed— forever changed at my very core.

*Each phase in my grief journey allows
me to explore where I am right now.
By accepting that I am where I must
need to be, I am free to live today.*

*The place I am today can become
friend instead of foe. The journey into
my loss has already created change,
and the present and future will create
more. Now may be the
time to examine my expectations of
myself, and accept that I am where
I need to be for now.*

*Part of healing in grief requires that
I listen to myself—to slow down,
to turn inward, to feel what I must
feel. Going into neutral ultimately
helps me encounter joy.*

Now I realize: I knew myself so little. This death has forced me to become reacquainted with myself. I must slow down and listen.

*Sometimes the business of life
becomes so full that I risk losing
myself in my daily living. The death
of someone I love further erodes my
identity, my sense of self in relation
to the world around me.*

*To heal I must do nothing. I must
turn inward. I must slow down. And
as I discover my emptiness, I must ask
myself: Who am I? How am I
changed by the death of this person?
Where am I going?*

*The active cultivation of my changed
self helps me discover a new depth,
beauty and richness in my life. My
need to mourn has caused me to step
back from the busyness of daily living.
As I learn to nurture my inner self,
I find a new appreciation for each
new day, each new relationship.*

My grief journey opens me to every level of my identity. The loss of a mirror to who I am sometimes fills me with overwhelming sadness: I am being transformed.

I face my new self and fear the unknown. Yet, as I open my heart, new light emerges and I am full of love. The more I come to understand the new "I," the more I have to give back to my life and to those I love.

I am finding that my new self honors,
indeed demands, contemplation.
Doing nothing allows me to turn
my attention to who I really am.

Why am I here? What is my purpose?
How can I lead a more
soul-centered life?

As I get acquainted with my new self, my soul celebrates being. Walking through the woods, reading a good book, sitting quietly with my child or my friend—all are times of retreat and rejuvenation.

*A vital part of healing my identity
is only a walk away.*

*Solitary hikes through the woods,
no need to get someplace, no rewards
for speed—simply going away—this is
the heart of retreat and renewal.*

Part of discovering my new self has been learning to listen, not talk.

Turning inward requires a silence, a quietness—not only on the outside, but on the inside. I just keep listening until I hear something.

Patience brings discovery of a new me. And as I listen, I begin to like what I hear.

*As I change I learn to retreat—
to say no to always staying connected
to a world outside of myself. This
art of pulling in ultimately creates a
newfound I, full of spiritual integrity
and overflowing with love.*

Withdrawal brings new life.

As I feel my sadness, I'm at times uncertain of who I am. This sadness calls out for me to impose periods of alone time—to discover my changed self. As I slowly venture back out into the world, I'm different, yet somehow I'm whole again.

Where I am in the grief journey alters how I see myself, my expectations, my dreams, my hopes. The time I have already been mourning has created a changed "I." Perhaps I need to adjust my personal self-expectations so they reflect where I am right now.

*When I have a commitment and
longing to find my changed self, I have
an alternative to the constant, blinding
pain of the loss. Discovering my
changed me clears a space to discover
new life. I have something to turn
toward instead of away from. I have
something to cry out for that releases
my inner tension. I have something
that is authentic, real: It is the life that
breaks through my loneliness, with a
direction and power of its own.
Welcome home.*

Death came without my permission.
While I know grief is universal,
it's just so hard to contemplate the
death of someone who brought
meaning to my life.

My life is in large part formed
by the people around me. Death
creates the obvious—living without
the presence of someone loved.
This dramatic change challenges
my character, my personhood.

Learning to survive my changed
life draws upon all my resources. I am
still capable of being loved and cared
for. I am still capable of living a life
of purpose and meaning.

MOURNING NEED

5

SEARCHING
FOR MEANING

When someone you love dies, you naturally question the meaning and purpose of life. You probably will question your philosophy of life and explore religious and spiritual values as you work on this need. You may discover yourself searching for meaning in your continued living as you ask "How" and "Why" questions.

"How could God let this happen?" "Why did this happen now, in this way?" The death reminds you of your lack of control. It can leave you feeling powerless.

The person who died was a part of you. This death means you mourn a loss not only outside of yourself, but inside of yourself as well. At times, overwhelming sadness and loneliness may be your constant companions. You may feel that when this person died, part of you died with him or her. And now you are faced with finding some meaning in going on with your life even though you may often feel so empty.

This death calls for you to confront your own spirituality. You may doubt your faith and have spiritual conflicts and questions racing through your head and heart. This is normal and part of your journey toward renewed living.

You might feel distant from your God or higher power, even questioning the very existence of God. You may rage at your God. Such feelings of doubt are normal. Remember—mourners often find themselves questioning their faith for months

before they rediscover meaning in life. But be assured: It can be done, even when you don't have all the answers.

Early in your grief, allow yourself to openly mourn without pressuring yourself to have answers to such profound "meaning of life" questions. Move at your own pace as you recognize that allowing yourself to hurt and finding meaning are not mutually exclusive. More often your need to mourn and find meaning in your continued living will blend into each other, with the former giving way to the latter as healing occurs.

The death of someone I love makes me examine where I am right now, today. The freshness of this death has the potential of freeing me from my focus on more time and inspires me to use this time.

To find renewed meaning in life,
I must commit to persevere. Perhaps
only through determination do I reach
a place within myself long enough
to awaken the desire to turn
toward the light of life.

*Self-understanding of this grief
journey only comes when I expand
myself to my fullest capacities and
accept myself just where I am.
Then and only then do I see
movement in my quest to live again.*

*Out of the depths of this grief comes
an inner clarity, a sense of purpose, an
internal richness, a warming of heart
and spirit that expresses itself in a
desire to love and be loved.*

*The very meaning of life can be
discovered in our daily relationships
and what passes among us. The loss
I have come to know calls out to me to
live awake and alive—to risk, to push
the boundaries of my potential—
not to look back with regret over
what might have been.*

*I must encounter my questions,
my doubts, my fears. There is richness
in these domains. As I explore them
I don't reinforce my tensions but
instead release them. In this way
I transcend my grief and discover new
life beyond anything my heart
could ever have comprehended.*

Oh, the gentleness of new life.

*The death of someone I love may be
the greatest pain I can endure, for it
signifies the end of what I have
known that made me feel safe.*

*This death is not just a physical loss
but a spiritual loss. At times I fear
that I cannot live through this loss,
but I can. I will.*

*As laughter gently reenters my life,
I come to rejoice: The deep despair
is not permanent. I choose life
as I keep memories alive!*

*I cannot "think through" my grief
journey. Intellectual concepts often
serve to obstruct me from myself.*

*Unless I can cross the bridge to
my heart I will never wake up
and be transformed.*

*To truly heal, I must become aware
of my emotional and spiritual selves.
I must not be distracted from peeling
myself away and cultivating a
true inner awareness.*

*Sometimes I wonder: Does laughter
have a place in my healing? Laughter
cleanses my soul and mends my heart.
It connects me to the world around
me. When I allow myself levity,
I discover I am alive.*

Rediscovering the capacity to experience joy and happiness in life is one of my ultimate goals. How I get there or if I get there depends on my ability to find meaning in my continued living.

In large part my happiness depends on me, not others. Now, more than ever, I must seek joyful moments to let me breathe. Experiencing joy helps me know I'm alive! I will close my eyes and embrace moments of happiness.

My grief journey has no one destination. I will not "get over it." The understanding that I don't have to be done is liberating. I will mourn this death for the rest of my life.

*As I search for meaning I don't have
to carry my burdens alone. Prayer,
if I allow it to, can crystallize in words
my hopes for continued life. If I have
forgotten how to pray, I can always
remember or relearn.*

*The reality of grief and its lingering
effects underscores the limited control
I have over many aspects of my life.
I have no power to bring those I love
back to life. Out of my helplessness
comes a need to find balance, hope
and healing. Perhaps in turning
to God I can find the comfort
I so desperately need.*

*I deserve to be proud of my search
for meaning in life after the death of
someone I love. Grief confronts me
with the reality that life is now.
Today. I can demonstrate the value
in my life and the lives of those who
have died before me by living
fully—today. By risking—today.
By letting people know
I love them—today.*

*To find meaning in continued living,
I must open my heart and invite
God in. He is there—waiting.
Patiently waiting day after day.
It is my openness to God that
transcends my grief and
transports my soul.*

Finding meaning in my grief and mourning is real work. As I discover my changed self, I experience uncertainty, disorientation, fear and even a newfound vulnerability. This experience challenges my assumptions about myself and my world.

The pain of loss teaches me so much about myself. It teaches me about the gift of loving and being loved. I must hold up this realization and honor it.

*This embracing of grief makes me
so aware of the preciousness of life.
While I see darkness in my grief,
to heal I must seek out light. I will
discover that life and living are sacred,
beautiful, gifts to be treasured each
and every moment.*

My spiritual understanding of life and death often grows at its own pace. It's not as if I can wake up one day and say, "Today I'll be spiritual and deeply connected to my higher power." What I can do is strive to create an open space in my heart and invite God in. Perhaps it is my openness to something greater than myself that underlies my grief journey, awakens my compassion to others in pain and allows me to become more of who I really am.

Working on my grief could be considered soul work. Death causes me to become more intimate with myself, others, and the world around me.

This journey is an education of my soul, and is manifested in the unfolding of new ways of seeing the world around me.

Healing in grief requires contemplation and turning inward. Quietness and emptiness invite the heart to observe signs of sacredness, to regain purpose, to rediscover love, to renew life!

When death comes and grief pervades each day, I sometimes question my capacity to survive. Yet, there is such quiet strength in my spiritual resources. Realizing this, I can move toward life again. I can move forward with an abiding faith and love.

*This death has made me look at
what is important in life.
How very important the choices
I make each moment are both to
myself and those I love.*

*I have discovered a new sense
of direction and purpose in my life.
I have reassessed my goals, reset
priorities, and become deeply
connected to those I love.*

When I feel battered by overwhelming grief, I can restore myself through solitude, quietness, and peace. Alone time allows my body, mind, and heart to be rejuvenated. The privacy of the moment allows me to discover the reason to live again.

*I sometimes feel overwhelmed by
the fear of an uncertain future. Will
I ever love and be loved like that
again? Whom can I turn to who will
help me find my way back from this
place? And then I remember: My
God is here for me, patiently waiting,
ready to comfort and support me.
Thank you, God, for loving me.*

I cannot escape this journey into grief,
this drain of my life force.

Yet, I can regenerate meaning and
purpose in my life. While I can't push
away my loss, I can have a hopeful
attitude toward my healing.
This is how I renew faith in myself,
my family and friends, and
the world around me.

Experiencing my grief is far more demanding than I ever imagined. Yet, I have discovered I have the capacity to convert the pain into purposeful expression by helping others. I will reach out to at least one person each day. As I help others, I also help myself.

MOURNING NEED

6

RECEIVING ONGOING SUPPORT FROM OTHERS

The quality and quantity of understanding support you get during your "work of mourning" will have a major influence on your capacity to heal. You cannot—nor should you try to—do this alone. Drawing on the experiences and encouragement of friends, fellow grieving people or professional counselors is not a weakness but a healthy human need. And because mourning is a process that takes place over time, this support must be available months and even years after the death of someone in your life.

Unfortunately, because our society places so much value on the ability to "carry on," "keep your chin up" and "keep busy," many mourners are abandoned shortly after the event of the death. "It's best not to talk about the death," "It's over and done with" and "It's time to get on with your life" are still the dominant types of messages directed at mourners. Obviously, these messages encourage you to deny or repress your grief rather than express it.

If you know people who consider themselves supportive yet offer you these kinds of "mourning avoiding" messages, you will need to look to others for truly helpful support. People who see your mourning as something that should be "overcome" instead of experienced will not help you heal.

To be truly helpful, the people in your support system must appreciate the impact this death has had on you. They must understand that in order to heal, you must be allowed—even encouraged—to mourn long after the death. And they must encourage you to see mourning not as an enemy to be vanquished but as a necessity to be experienced as a result of having loved.

I may have fears about reentering the world of other people. If I'm not careful, my fears may immobilize me from taking risks and venturing out into the world again.

My best opportunity for healing, despite the pain of the loss I have experienced, is to develop a hopeful attitude, an open nature, and a willingness to surround myself with those who support and love me.

Reaching out to others may not protect me from my fears, but it does create a loving bond with human beings who genuinely care about me.

*I will be well-served to be gracious
to those who reach out to help me.
Yes, sometimes they say the
wrong things; they are often
well-intended but misinformed.*

*If I am not careful, I may find
myself pushing away those who want
to help me. In receiving support I am
forced to acknowledge my losses.*

*The turmoil of my grief leaves
me raw, on edge, vulnerable. I may
refuse support because of pride,
unaware that in keeping people
away I delay my ultimate healing.*

*Grace means letting people in—
allowing myself to touch
and be touched.*

As I journey toward healing,
I must help myself. One avenue to
help myself is to reach out to a
support group. A group can offer me a
"safe place," a shared commonality
of experience and a hope
for inner healing.

*I need not instinctively know what
to do or how to be with my grief.
I can reach out to others who have
walked this path before. I learn that
to ultimately heal, I must touch and
be touched by the experiences of those
who have gone before me. These
people can offer me hope, inner
strength and the gift of love.*

The secret to healing in grief is very clear: the love and support of people who surround me with compassion. This love is the antidote to my pain. It is an acceptance of this love that engages my desire to go on living.

I have never known pain like this before. It overwhelms me. As I adapt, change and grow, I am entitled to be proud of my progress. As my grief changes I reflect on where I have been and where I am going. I do this best in the company of others.

I heal, in part, by allowing others to express their love for me. By choosing to invite others into my journey, I move toward health and healing. If I hide from others, I hide from healing.

*Very simply, if I want to live again,
I must seek support, understanding
and guidance. Being lost doesn't
mean I have to stay lost.*

Part of healing means expressing myself publicly again. It takes courage, self-love and determination to move from the inward position of necessary retreat to the outward position of necessary risk. Yet, to venture out enhances my ability to live again.

*If I am full of grief, expressing it
will empty me out. The capacity to
experience emptiness will allow me to
begin to fill up with life again.
As I begin to fill up, I need caring
people to continue to support
and understand me.*

Expressing my grief outwardly affirms my need to mourn—to expand beyond my inner self, to invite others into my space. I cannot do this alone.

*Paradoxically, as a mourner
I need daily retreat to enable me to be
a part of community, family, and the
world around me. I pull back in
silence, I pray without specific goals,
I walk alone in the darkness.*

*I withdraw so I can slowly reemerge
and become whole again.*

As I experience my grief, I'm pulled to be both alone and together with others. I realize I need both. The beauty of it is that I have discovered I can embrace both needs. One does not preclude the other. What an important revelation!

Sometimes I try to do it all on my own. This can actually put me into a state of numbness, causing retreat from the world around me. I can turn to others for help when I need it. I can do this because it is a self-compassionate, deserving, loving way to be.

The Journey Through Grief:
An Epilogue

You may have heard—indeed you may believe—that your grief journey's end will come when you resolve, or recover from, your grief. But you may also be coming to understand one of the fundamental truths of grief: Your journey will never end. People do not "get over" grief. My personal and professional experience tells me that a total return to "normalcy" after the death of someone loved is not possible; we are all forever changed by the experience of grief.

Reconciliation is a term I find more appropriate for what occurs as the mourner works to integrate the new reality of moving forward in life without the physical presence of the person who died. With reconciliation comes a renewed sense of energy and confidence, an ability to fully acknowledge the reality of the death and a capacity to become reinvolved in the activities of living. There is also an acknowledgment that pain and grief are difficult, yet necessary, parts of life.

As the experience of reconciliation unfolds, you will recognize that life is and will continue to be different without the presence of the person who died. Changing the relationship with the person who died from one of presence to one of memory and redirecting one's energy and initiative toward the future often takes longer—and involves more hard work—than most people are aware. We, as human beings, never resolve our grief, but instead become reconciled to it.

We come to reconciliation in our grief journeys when the full reality of the death becomes a part of us. Beyond an intellectual working through of the death, there is also an emotional and spiritual working through. What had been understood at the "head" level is now understood at the "heart" level.

In reconciliation, the sharp, ever-present pain of grief gives rise to a renewed sense of meaning and purpose. Your feelings of loss will not completely disappear, yet they will soften, and the intense pangs of grief will become less frequent. Hope for a continued life will emerge as you are able to make commitments to the future, realizing that the person you have given love to and received love from will never be forgotten. The unfolding of this journey is not intended to create a return to an "old normal" but the discovery of a "new normal."

GROWTH THROUGH GRIEF: THE POSSIBILITIES!

Happily, you may well also find that you are growing emotionally and spiritually as a result of your journey. But before I say more about growth through grief, a caveat: Though grief can indeed transform into growth, I would never seek out the pain of grief in an effort to experience growth. While our "greatest gifts often come from our wounds," these are not wounds we masochistically go looking for. When others offer ill-timed, mis-stated comments like "You'll grow from this," our right to hurt is taken away from us. We must allow all mourners to discover on their own the ways in which they will grow through grief, perhaps gently encouraging them at times but never taking away their need—indeed their right—to be angry, scared or deeply sad.

Growth means a new inner balance with no end points

While you may do the work of mourning to recapture in part some sense of inner balance, it is a new inner balance. My hope is that the term growth reflects the fact that we never reach some end point in our grief journeys.

No one ever totally completes the mourning process. People who think you get over grief are often continually striving to "pull it all together," while at the same time feeling that something is missing. How would you describe your new inner balance?

Growth means exploring our assumptions about life

Growth in grief is a lifelong process of exploring how death challenges us to look at our assumptions about life. When someone loved dies, we naturally question the meaning and purpose of life. Religious and spiritual values also come under scrutiny. We might ask questions like, "How can God let this happen?" or "Why did this happen now—to me?" Many times we also ask ourselves why we should go on living.

Finding answers to these questions is a long and arduous process. But ultimately, exploring our assumptions about life after the death of someone loved can make those assumptions richer and more life-affirming. We often achieve a greater understanding of our spirituality, for example. We may discover a shift in life priorities and find a personal, inner peace we lacked before. For me, growth in grief is a lifelong process of exploring how death challenges us to look at our assumptions about life. How have your assumptions been changed?

Growth means utilizing our potentials

The encounter of grief reawakens us to the importance of utilizing our potentials—our capacities to mourn our losses openly and without shame, to be interpersonally effective in our relationships with others, and to continue to discover fulfillment in life, living and loving. Rather than "dragging us down," loss often helps us grow. Loss seems to free the potential within. Then it becomes up to us as human beings to embrace and creatively express this potential. Have you found yourself using your potential in new ways?

Obviously, not every mourner experiences the kind of actualizing growth I have just described. Unfortunately, some people do not seem to know how to grow. They remain emotionally, physically and spiritually crippled for years. Instead of being changed in a positive way, they have gone backward or regressed. The forces of grief have seemed to work against them instead of for them.

In fact, in our "mourning-avoiding" culture, more and more people are invited *not* to grow in their grief journeys. Our challenge as mourners, then, is to fight this cultural tendency and instead discover how this experience can enrich our lives. We must learn to free ourselves to grow and live until we die.

A final word to those who journey

It is important to me that you know my thoughts and prayers are with you. Yes, it takes courage to face your real feelings. It takes patience to discover life again. And it takes self-compassion to believe that experiencing the six needs explored in this book will help your pain soften over time.

I believe we are well served to remember those familiar words, "Blessed are those who mourn, for they shall be comforted" and "How happy are those who know what sorrow means, for they will be given courage and comfort."

Sometimes it is difficult to see mourning as an asset in life. Yet, the capacity to love requires the necessity to mourn. We must come to understand that we are not being self-indulgent but instead self-sustaining.

I truly hope this book has served as a loving companion to you. I believe you can and will go on to discover renewed meaning and purpose in your life, in your living and in your loving!

Just one more thing: Right now, take a moment to close your eyes, open your heart, and remember the precious smile of the person in your life who has died.

Thank you for letting me be a small part of your healing. I hope we meet one day.

THE MOURNER'S CODE:
TEN INALIENABLE RIGHTS
AS YOU JOURNEY THROUGH GRIEF

Though you should reach out to others as you journey through grief, you should not feel obligated to accept the unhelpful responses you may receive from some people. You are the one who is grieving, and as such, you have certain "rights" no one should try to take away from you.

The following list is intended both to empower you to heal and to decide how others can and cannot help. This is not to discourage you from reaching out to others for help, but rather to assist you in distinguishing useful responses from hurtful ones.

1. *You have the right to experience your own unique grief.*

   No one else will grieve in exactly the same way you do. So, when you turn to others for help, don't allow them to tell you what you should or should not be feeling.

2. *You have the right to talk about your grief.*

   Talking about your grief will help you heal. Seek out others who will allow you to talk as much as you want, as often as you want, about your grief. If at times you don't feel like talking, you also have the right to be silent.

3. *You have the right to feel
   a multitude of emotions.*

   Confusion, disorientation, fear, guilt and relief
   are just a few of the emotions you might feel
   as part of your grief journey. Others may try to
   tell you that feeling angry, for example, is
   wrong. Don't take these judgmental responses
   to heart. Instead, find listeners who will accept
   your feelings without condition.

4. *You have the right to be tolerant of your physical
   and emotional limits.*

   Your feelings of loss and sadness will probably
   leave you feeling fatigued. Respect what your
   body and mind are telling you. Get daily rest.
   Eat balanced meals. And don't allow others to
   push you into doing things you don't feel
   ready to do.

5. *You have the right to experience "griefbursts."*

   Sometimes, out of nowhere, a powerful surge
   of grief may overcome you. This can be
   frightening, but it is normal and natural. Find
   someone who understands and will let you
   talk it out.

6. *You have the right to make use of ritual.*

   The funeral ritual does more than acknowledge the death of someone loved. It helps
   provide you with the support of caring people.
   More importantly, the funeral is a way for you
   to mourn. If others tell you the funeral or
   other healing rituals such as these are silly or
   unnecessary, don't listen.

7. *You have the right to embrace your spirituality.*

   If faith is a part of your life, express it in ways
   that seem appropriate to you. Allow yourself
   to be around people who understand and
   support your religious beliefs. If you feel angry
   at God, find someone to talk with who won't
   be critical of your feelings of hurt and
   abandonment.

8. *You have the right to search for meaning.*

   You may find yourself asking, "Why did he or
   she die? Why this way? Why now?" Some of
   your questions may have answers, but some
   may not. And watch out for the clichéd
   responses some people may give you.
   Comments like, "It was God's will" or
   "Think of what you still have to be thankful
   for" are not helpful and you do not have to
   accept them.

9. *You have the right to treasure your memories.*

Memories are one of the best legacies that exist after the death of someone loved. You will always remember. Instead of ignoring your memories, find others with whom you can share them.

10. *You have the right to move toward your grief and heal.*

Reconciling your grief will not happen quickly. Remember, grief is best experienced in "doses." Be patient and tolerant with yourself and avoid people who are impatient and intolerant with you. Neither you nor those around you must forget that the death of someone loved changes your life forever.

Also by Alan D. Wolfelt, Ph.D.

Additional Resources for Adult Mourners

Understanding Grief: Helping Yourself Heal

A compassionate guide to coping with the death of someone loved, this bestseller helps bereaved people move toward healing by encouraging them to explore their unique journeys into grief and mourning.

Chapter titles include:

- Common Myths About Grief and Mourning
- My Grief is Unique
- What Might I Expect?
- How Am I Doing?
- Taking Care of Myself
- Do I Need Additional Help?
- Helping Guidelines for Support Groups (including a nine-session support group model based on this text)
- Helping a Friend in Grief.

Throughout, readers are asked specific questions about their grief journeys and encouraged to think about and write down their responses. Since its publication in 1992, *Understanding Grief* has been Dr. Wolfelt's most well-known, well-loved book for mourners. Everyone who grieves deserves the support and companionship of this popular, compassionate book.

200 pages. Softcover. $18.95
(plus additional shipping and handling)

All Dr. Wolfelt's publications can be ordered by mail from:

Companion Press
3735 Broken Bow Road • Fort Collins, CO 80526
(970) 226-6050 • Fax 1-800-922-6051

All prices are in U.S. dollars and are valid through December, 1997.

How to Reach Out for Help When You Are Grieving

This beautifully designed booklet compassionately addresses mourners and encourages them to seek support from others. Topics include:

- The Grieving Person's Bill of Rights
- Where to Turn for Help
- How to Know if You Need Professional Help
- Individual Counseling (including how to find a good counselor)
- Support Groups
- Assessing Your Progress

  and more. A concise, practical guide to the whys and hows of seeking support from others in times of grief.

33 pages. $5.00
($3.00 each when ordered in quantities of 25 or more)
(plus additional shipping and handling)

All Dr. Wolfelt's publications can be ordered by mail from:

Companion Press
3735 Broken Bow Road • Fort Collins, CO 80526
(970) 226-6050 • Fax 1-800-922-6051

All prices are in U.S. dollars and are valid through December, 1997.

Healing the Bereaved Child: Grief Gardening, Growth Through Grief and Other Touchstones for Caregivers

This inspiring, heartfelt book for caregivers to bereaved children contains chapter after chapter of practical caregiving guidelines:

- How a grieving child thinks, feels and mourns
- What makes each child's grief unique
- How the bereaved child heals: the six needs of mourning
- Foundations of counseling bereaved children
- Counseling techniques (play, art, writing, nature and many others; more than 45 pages!)
- A family systems approach to counseling
- Support groups for bereaved kids, including a 10-session model
- Helping grieving children at school, including a crisis response team model
- Helping the grieving adolescent
- Self-care for the child's bereavement caregiver

Part textbook, part workbook, part meditation, this bestselling guide is a must-read for child counselors, hospice caregivers, funeral directors, school counselors and teachers, clergy, parents—anyone who wants to offer support and companionship to children affected by the death of someone loved.

8 ½" x 11" format, 344 pages. Softcover. $39.95
(plus additional shipping and handling)

All Dr. Wolfelt's publications can be ordered by mail from:

Companion Press
3735 Broken Bow Road • Fort Collins, CO 80526
(970) 226-6050 • Fax 1-800-922-6051

All prices are in U.S. dollars and are valid through December, 1997.

How I Feel
A Coloring Book for Grieving Children

Dr. Wolfelt's coloring book for kids ages 3-8 explores many of the feelings grieving children often experience. The expressive, easy-to-color drawings clearly depict disbelief, fear, anger, loneliness, happiness, sadness and other normal grief feelings.

24 pages $1.00
(plus $2 S&H per individual copy; bulk pricing and shipping available)

My Grief Rights
A poster for grieving children

This colorful, oversized poster helps grieving kids understand their feelings and empowers them to mourn in healthy ways. Sample headings: I have the right to my own unique feelings about the death; I have the right to need other people to help me with my grief, especially grown-ups who care about me.

Poster (24" x 36") $10.00
(plus additional shipping and handling)

A Child's View of Grief

In this informative, easy-to-read booklet, Dr. Wolfelt explains how children and adolescents grieve after someone loved dies and offers helping guidelines for caregiving adults. A concise resource for parents of grieving kids. The companion videotape, written by and featuring Dr. Wolfelt as well as actual bereaved children and their families, explores several key principles of helping children cope with grief.

Booklet 45 pages. Softcover. $5.95
Videotape 20 minutes. $64.95
(plus additional shipping and handling)

Resources for and about Grieving Children and Teenagers

What Bereaved Children Want Adults to Know About Grief

A Companion Press classic, this booklet and audio-cassette package offer 15 Principles About Grief and Children and then describe them in language a grieving child might actually use. In the cassette, Dr. Wolfelt's teachings about the 15 principles are interspersed with comments from actual bereaved kids.

35-page, pocket-sized booklet and 25-minute audiocassette.
$15.95   *(plus additional shipping and handling)*

Sarah's Journey

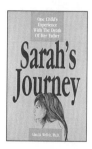

Eight-year-old Sarah had always been her "daddy's lit-tle girl"—until the tragic day her father was killed in a car accident. Based on the belief that each child needs to mourn in her own way, this book describes Sarah's grief experience and offers compassionate, practical advice for adults on topics such as regressive behaviors, explosive emotions, children and funerals, the grieving child at school and more.

121 pages. Softcover. $9.95
(plus additional shipping and handling)

A Teen's View of Grief

An Educational Videotape for Bereavement Caregivers

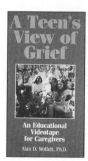

This fresh video on teen grief, written by and featuring Dr. Wolfelt, explodes with in-depth information in its beautifully produced forty minutes: adolescent tasks complicated by grief, nature of the deaths encountered by teens, the grieving teen's support systems and mourning needs, signs a teen may need extra help and practical helping guidelines. Throughout, Dr. Wolfelt's teachings are interspersed with comments from actual bereaved teens.

40-minute videotape $99.95
(plus additional shipping and handling)

All Dr. Wolfelt's publications can be ordered by mail from:

Companion Press
3735 Broken Bow Road • Fort Collins, CO 80526
(970) 226-6050 • Fax 1-800-922-6051

All prices are in U.S. dollars and are valid through December, 1997.

Creating Meaningful Funeral Ceremonies: A Guide for Caregivers

Written in an attempt to counteract the current North American trend to deritualize death and to reinstill in us a respect for meaningful funeral rituals, this bestselling booklet explores the ways in which heartfelt funeral ceremonies help the bereaved begin to heal. It also reviews qualities in caregivers that make them effective funeral planners and provides practical ideas for creating authentic, personalized and meaningful funeral ceremonies. An inspiring guide for clergy and others who help grieving families plan and carry out funerals.

65 pages. Softcover. $12.95
(plus additional shipping and handling)

How to Care for Yourself While You Care for the Dying and the Bereaved

Do you need some practice taking better care of yourself? Dr. Wolfelt has written this practical booklet on the importance and the practice of self-care for caregivers to the dying and the bereaved:

- why excellent self-care is essential
- the art of erasing "worktapes"
- caregiver fatigue syndrome
- the overcaring caregiver
- the bereavement caregiver's self-care guidelines.

Makes an excellent gift for your staff members, your community's caregivers or, of course, yourself!

33-pages. Softcover. $10.00
(plus additional shipping and handling)

All Dr. Wolfelt's publications can be ordered by mail from:

Companion Press
3735 Broken Bow Road • Fort Collins, CO 80526
(970) 226-6050 • Fax 1-800-922-6051

All prices are in U.S. dollars and are valid through December, 1997.

How to Start and Lead a Bereavement Support Group

For professional caregivers as well as interested laypeople, this oversized booklet details step-by-step instructions for starting and effectively leading a bereavement support group. Includes a nine-session meeting plan.

48 pages. Softcover. $10.00
(plus additional shipping and handling)

The Helping Series

Concise brochures written by Dr. Wolfelt and designed for economical mass distribution, the Helping Series offers assistance to the bereaved in coping with specific types of death and grief responses. In use by hundreds of hospices and funeral homes throughout North America. Sample titles include:

Helping a **Friend in Grief**

Helping **Children** Cope with Grief

Helping a **Suicide Survivor** Heal

Helping **SIDS Survivors** Heal

Helping **Teenagers** Cope with Grief

Helping Yourself Heal During the **Holiday Season**

Helping Yourself Heal When a **Parent Dies**

Helping **Yourself Heal** When Someone Dies

Helping Yourself Heal **When Your Spouse Die**s

Our Helping Series sample packet contains one each of 26 titles, allowing you to read through all the brochures and select those most appropriate for your organization or clientele. Each sample packet also includes complete bulk pricing and ordering information for subsequent Helping Series orders.

Helping Series sample packet • $10.00
(plus additional shipping and handling)

All Dr. Wolfelt's publications can be ordered by mail from:

Companion Press
3735 Broken Bow Road • Fort Collins, CO 80526
(970) 226-6050 • Fax 1-800-922-6051

All prices are in U.S. dollars and are valid through December, 1997.